Stratford Library Association
2203 Main Street
Stratford, CT 06615
203-385-4160

 **W9-DES-298**

YOU WRITE IT!

BY
JOHN HAMILTON

Published by ABDO Publishing Company, 8000 West 78th Street, Suite 310, Edina, Minnesota 55439.
Copyright ©2009 by Abdo Consulting Group, Inc. International copyrights reserved in all countries.
No part of this book may be reproduced in any form without written permission from the publisher.
ABDO & Daughters™ is a trademark and logo of ABDO Publishing Company.

Printed in the United States.

Editor: Sue Hamilton
Graphic Design: Sue Hamilton
Cover Design: Neil Klinepier
Cover Illustration: Background image, Don Maitz; Foreground image, iStock
Interior Photos and Illustrations: p 1 Horror art, Corbis; p 3 Skull and candle, iStock; p 4 Skull
and books, iStock; Browsing in the dark, iStock; p 5 Woman writing horror story, iStock; p 6 Girl
thinking, Comstock; p 7 Boy reading book, iStock; p 8 Typewriter, iStock; p 9 Woman overloaded
with work, iStock; p 10 Teen working on laptop, iStock; Actor as vampire, iStock; p 11 Index card,
iStock; p 12 Monster, iStock; p 13 Moonlight walk art, Getty Images; p 14 Van Helsing wax figure,
Getty Images; p 15 Vampire and zombie, AP Images; p 16 *Aliens* creature, courtesy Twentieth
Century Fox; p 17 Henry Hull from *Werewolf of London*, Corbis; p 18 Girl working, iStock; Post-it
Note, iStock; p 19 Man holding keyboard, iStock; pp 20-23 Picture stills from *I Am Legend*, courtesy
Warner Bros. Pictures; p 22 Notebook, iStock; p 24 Girl happy by computer, iStock; p 25 Christopher
Lee in *Dracula A.D. 1972*, Getty Images; p 26 *H.P. Lovecraft's Magazine of Horror*, courtesy Wildside
Press; p 27 Teen holding typewriter, iStock; p 28 Stephen King novels, courtesy Random House
Publishing; Stephen King portrait, courtesy Stephen King; p 29 R.L. Stine portrait, AP Images; Dean
Koontz portrait, Getty Images; p 32 Scared couple, Comstock.

Library of Congress Cataloging-in-Publication Data

Hamilton, John, 1959-
  You write it : horror / John Hamilton.
      p. cm. -- (You write it!)
  Includes bibliographical references and index.
  ISBN 978-1-60453-506-8
  1. Horror tales--Authorship--Juvenile literature. I. Title.

PN3377.5.H67H36 2009
808.3'8738--dc22

                                2008044316

CONTENTS

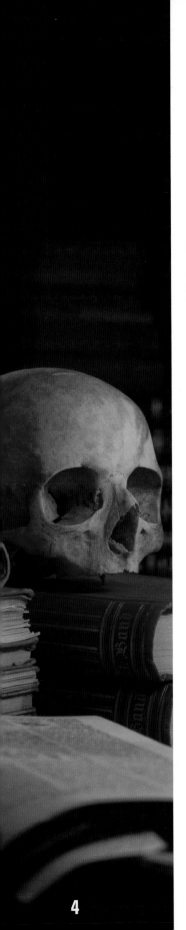

INTRODUCTION

"We make up horrors to help us cope with the real ones."
—Stephen King

What is horror, and why do we enjoy reading it so much? The dictionary says horror is a feeling of intense fear or dread. Classic monsters such as werewolves and zombies bring out these fearful feelings. But a horror story doesn't need supernatural beasts in order to frighten readers. Any story that creates emotions of fear and dread can technically be called horror. The genre can be about anything that people are afraid of: creepy teachers, drive-by shooters, politicians. In fact, many people object to horror being called a genre, or category of fiction. Elements of horror can be found in almost all kinds of writing.

At its core, horror reflects our fear of the unknown. Reading tales about vampires and ghosts helps us make sense of serious, unknowable questions: What happens when we die? Is there an afterlife? Can people come back from the dead?

Perhaps *you've* got a horror story you're dying to tell. But where to start? Novelist Gene Fowler once said, "Writing is easy. All you do is stare at a blank sheet of paper until drops of blood form on your forehead." What he meant is that writing is much harder than it looks. Anybody who can form a simple sentence thinks they can write. But good writing, like any other skill, takes practice.

Few people are born writers. However, there are certain skills anyone can learn. These "tools of the trade" can help you master the *craft* of writing. And once you've mastered the craft, you're well on your way to writing horror stories that others will love. You will encounter many obstacles along the way, but good writers find a way. The important thing is persistence, and a burning desire to tell your story.

Above: What story do you have to tell? A tale of a creepy teacher? A scientist who takes an experimental potion? Start writing your own horror story.

IDEAS

"Every book has some real life in it. I was never pursued by an evil twin clone, but everything else in Mr. Murder *was pretty much out of my own life."*

—Dean Koontz

The number one question asked of many horror writers is, where do you get your ideas? It's usually asked by insecure beginners who are afraid they don't have the imagination it takes to be successful. But as you'll soon find out, ideas are everywhere: in your head, in a book of fairy tales, in a stray conversation overheard at lunch. Developing an idea into a *story* is where the hard work takes place.

The reason we read, and write, horror stories is to deal with the unknown, especially big issues like death. It's practice for dealing with death in real life. The job of the horror writer is to not look away, to find a kernel of truth in our characters' reactions to the horrible things they must wade through.

What frightens you the most? Is it the death of someone you care about? Your own death? Or maybe you're scared of suffering, perhaps from an illness or injury. Reading and writing about fictional characters who deal with these issues helps us prepare for such hardships in our real lives. This is called catharsis, a release of real emotion through the experience of drama.

Coming Up With Ideas

- You must *read* in order to write. Read a lot. Every day. But don't limit yourself to horror fiction. Elements of horror can also be found in most kinds of fiction.

- Write what you know. Use your past experiences, then translate them into ideas. What's the worst thing that's ever happened to you? How did you deal with it? What lessons did you learn that can come out in your fiction?

- Brainstorm. Time yourself for two minutes. Jot down any ideas that pop into your head. Don't edit yourself, even if you think the ideas are stupid. They may spark even more creativity later.

- Keep a daily journal. It can be like a diary or a blog, but it can also include ideas that pop into your head, drawings, articles, photos, etc. As you collect information, you'll see patterns begin to emerge of things that interest you the most. Explore these themes.

- Write down your dreams. And your daydreams.

Right: To be a good writer, you must read. Read every day.

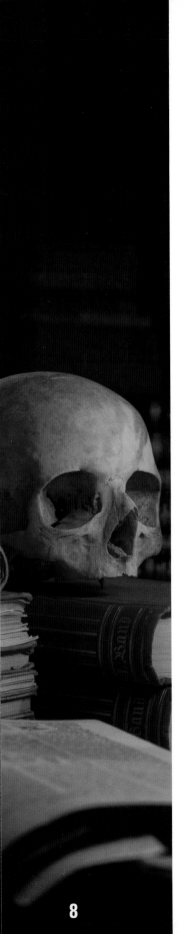

WORK HABITS

"Work every day. No matter what has happened the day or night before, get up and bite on the nail."

—Ernest Hemingway

Established writers will tell you over and over, the only way to learn to write is to write every day. It bears repeating: write… every… day. You wouldn't hire a carpenter to build your house unless he or she had a lot of practice in the craft, right? Do you think Michael Phelps broke swimming speed records the first time he jumped in a pool? Of course not! He spent thousands of hours in the water refining and perfecting his technique before he won his first gold medal. Writing is like any other craft or sport: it takes practice.

Find your own special place to write, a place where you can work uninterrupted. You can't wait for the mood to strike. You have to make time, even if you're busy. J.K. Rowling famously wrote much of *Harry Potter and the Sorcerer's Stone* in neighborhood cafes. (Her baby fell asleep during walks, so she ducked into cafes to take advantage of precious writing time.) If you have a laptop, you might think you can write anywhere. But it's usually best to find a single place to write. A desk in your bedroom might do, especially if you can close the door.

Or maybe a corner table in the library, or a quiet nook in a coffee shop. Think of it as your home base. Psychologically, it will help you tune out the world and get down to the business of writing.

Friends and family can be a terrible distraction. Even a minor interruption can stall your creativity. Enlist their help by making clear to them that you need to be left alone during your writing time. It doesn't always work, of course. But as you become a more practiced writer, it will take you less and less time to recover from life's inevitable distractions.

Don't Plagiarize

Writers are creative people. They want to bring their own ideas to life and share them with the world. Sometimes, though, deadline pressure (or sheer laziness) causes people to plagiarize others' work. Stealing somebody else's writing is a terrible idea. Not only is it totally wrong, it can bring you serious trouble. You can be suspended from school, expelled from college, or fired from a job. Don't do it! Besides, the world wants to read what springs from *your* mind, not somebody else's.

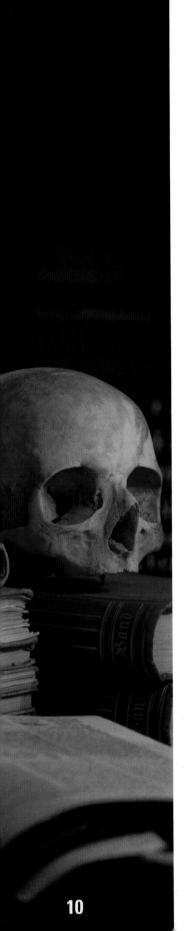

CHARACTER CREATION

"First, find out what your hero wants, then just follow him!"
—Ray Bradbury

What's more important, plot or character? Some writers say plot. After all, your readers are expecting a good story. On the other hand, think of the best books you've ever read. Chances are, what you remember most are the interesting characters, like Stephen King's Carrie, or Bram Stoker's Count Dracula.

The truth is, both plot and character are critical to good storytelling. You can't have one without the other. The reason characters are so memorable is because they are the key to unlocking the emotions of your story. You empathize with them, feel what they feel. Through great characters, you have an emotional stake in the outcome of the story. If you don't care about the characters, why should you care how the story turns out?

Right: Interesting characters are what readers remember.

Character Biographies

Good writers are people watchers. Study the people you meet every day. Start a character journal; write down what makes these people interesting to you. Observe their physical characteristics and their behavior. What quirks do they have? How do they dress? How do they walk and talk? Mold and twist these traits into your own fictional characters.

Many writers find it helpful to create very detailed biographies of all their major characters. This sometimes helps you to discover your characters' strengths and weaknesses, which you can use later when you throw them into the boiling stew of your plot.

Backstory is the history you create for your characters. Most of it may never make it into your final draft, but it helps make your characters seem more "real" as you write.

Character Biography Checklist

Below is a list of traits you might want to answer for each of your characters. You should at least know this backstory information for your hero and main villain. What other traits can you think of that will round out your characters' biographies? Get to know your main characters at least as well as you know your best friends.

Character Biography Checklist

- ✓ Character's full name
- ✓ Nickname
- ✓ Age/Birthdate
- ✓ Color of eyes/hair
- ✓ Height/weight
- ✓ Ethnic background
- ✓ Physical imperfections
- ✓ Glasses/contacts
- ✓ Family background
- ✓ Spouse/children
- ✓ Religion
- ✓ Politics
- ✓ School
- ✓ Special skills
- ✓ Military
- ✓ Job/profession
- ✓ Hobbies/sports
- ✓ Bad habits
- ✓ Fears
- ✓ Hopes and dreams

Character is Action

Characters are revealed through their actions. Instead of telling us that a ghost-hunter is brave, show him walking through a cemetery at night without a flashlight. Don't say that a monster is powerful; show him leaping straight up out of a deep pit. The point is, it's always better to reveal your characters' personalities through their behavior. Let their actions speak for themselves. It's one of the basic rules of fiction: show, don't tell.

Viewpoint

Whose "voice" is telling your story? The vast majority of fiction uses one of two viewpoints: first person and third person. First-person viewpoint uses the "I" voice, as if the reader were experiencing the action personally. *("I didn't always behave this way, quaking at the slightest movement or whisper of the wind. But after that night in the old, abandoned Johnson house, I'd never be the same.")* First person can be used very effectively to inhabit the thoughts and feelings of your main character. However, in first person your readers know only what your main character knows. This can sometimes limit your book, unless you are a very skilled storyteller.

On the other hand, third-person viewpoint (often called "third-person omniscient," or "the eye of God") lets you describe things your main character might not be aware of. You can describe your characters' feelings, but you can also take a step back and view the action from a more distant, neutral viewpoint.

(*A swirling fog wrapped its arms around a section of dark forest in the Carpathian foothills. As the moon shimmered down, lighting the mist like sheets of white satin, a ghostly apparition emerged from the fog. It floated slowly over a pair of train tracks, which stretched off into the distance, up into the snow-covered mountains. The apparition moved along the tracks, emitting a low, wailing noise as it went.*) For beginning writers, third-person viewpoint is a good choice. It has fewer pitfalls and complications.

Short stories almost always use a single viewpoint throughout. In longer forms, like novels, some authors like to mix up viewpoints for variety. Varying viewpoints can be very entertaining, but remember to keep the same viewpoint in each scene. Otherwise, you'll confuse your reader.

Heroes

The hero is your main character, or protagonist. He or she is the person the story is about. It's through the hero that readers experience your story, and make an emotional connection with the other characters.

Horror stories may seem like they're about weird, frightening events. But horror stories are *really* about how heroes react. Know your hero inside and out. How will he or she deal with the gruesome events you throw their way? How will the hero have to change to overcome the evil that threatens? What kind of person is this hero, anyway?

Above: A hero, such as the vampire-hunter Van Helsing, needs to connect with the reader.

Whatever kind of hero you choose, keep in mind one important thing: he or she should be reasonably likable. Readers will quickly abandon your book if your hero is disagreeable. To make your hero likeable, make him or her a capable person. The hero should be competent enough to solve the crime on his own, without calling in the cavalry. Give him a likeable trait or two. And be sure to give him a personal stake in the story. The reader will be much more engaged if the hero is personally threatened by the villain in some way.

Also, don't forget to give your heroes some flaws to overcome. This makes them seem more human, and interesting. Readers will root for a hero if they can relate to their fears and insecurities.

The Villain

The villain is the antagonist of the story, the one who tries to keep your hero from accomplishing his or her goal. Villains can be great fun to write. Many villains in horror stories are pure evil, since the point of these tales is the struggle of good versus evil. But the most effective villains

Above: From aliens to zombies, the best villains are evil, but charming.

have weaknesses and motivations we can relate to. Nobody's afraid of a villain who's all bluster and anger. But create a villain who seems like someone we could bump into on the street, and you've created something special.

An effective technique is to make your villains charming. It's what the villains use to lure their innocent victims, including your readers. Charming villains are villains we love to hate.

Of course, in many horror stories the villains are monsters. Still, that doesn't mean they can't be interesting. What motivates a monster to stalk its prey? Is it hungry? Or defending its territory? Or seeking revenge? If you give your monster motivation, it makes the peril seem more real. Plus, it gives your hero something to chew on when he tries to figure out how to defeat the beast.

Secondary Characters

Horror stories are populated by a rich variety of secondary characters. They help your hero overcome the problems you throw in his way. Many types of secondary characters show up again and again in stories. Joseph Campbell, the great scholar of mythology, identified characters who have common purposes. He called them archetypes, a kind of common personality trait first identified by psychologist Carl Jung.

A *mentor*, or "wise old man or woman," gives critical help or knowledge to the hero. In Stephen King's *The Shining*, Hallorann the cook warns the caretaker's boy Danny about the evil that resides in the Overlook Hotel.

Threshold guardians, also called gatekeeper guardians, are characters who test the hero, preparing him or her to battle the main villain later in the story. In the film *Aliens*, the hideous creatures battling the space marines are merely threshold guardians, like worker bees. The main villain appears late in the film, the gigantic alien queen that battles Ripley, the hero.

An *Aliens* creature.

Tricksters are helper characters who can be mischievous even as they assist the hero. Sometimes these characters are sidekicks who provide comic relief in contrast to the serious hero. A story that is serious all the time can be exhausting, especially horror stories. Unfortunately for tricksters in horror stories, they are often eaten by the monster.

How will you create and use your secondary characters? You might want to create character biographies the way you did with your hero and villain. You should at least know what motivates them. How are they critical to the story, and why do they act the way they do?

Silver bullets?!

Dialogue

Good dialogue propels the story. If you simply restate the obvious, then your dialogue is too "on the nose." After describing a werewolf rampaging through a group of helpless villagers, you probably don't need a character to point to the beast and say, "Look out! A werewolf!" Instead, have him say something that also reveals his character. A hero might demonstrate his quick-thinking skills by crying out, "Fetch my gun! It's loaded with silver bullets!" In addition to giving information, good dialogue adds mood and suspense.

When writing dialogue speech verbs, a simple "he said" or "she said" is best. Too many beginning writers clutter their dialogue with unnecessary adverbs in order to show a character's emotions: *"You'll never leave this tomb alive," the vampire said menacingly.* So, what's so bad about "menacingly"? It's much better to *show* action instead of using an adverb. For example: *The vampire leaned over and smiled, droplets of blood dripping from his teeth. "You'll never leave this tomb alive," he said.* Even though the writer simply used the word "said," the vampire's menacing tone is unmistakable.

Start a dialogue notebook. Write down speech you overhear at home, during lunch hour, or at the mall. You'll quickly discover that real speech is very different from written dialogue. Real speech often overlaps, and is filled with "ums," "ers," and "likes." Written dialogue should not mimic real speech; real speech on the page quickly becomes tedious.

Write down interesting figures of speech you overhear. Idioms like "they were thick as thieves" or "kick the bucket" can be great for creating interesting characters. But be sparing when writing regional dialects. A little goes a long way.

PLOTS

"Fiction is a lie, and good fiction is the truth inside the lie."
—Stephen King

Planning a piece of fiction, especially a long piece like a novel, can be a daunting task. It becomes more manageable if you break it down into smaller parts. You've probably already learned in school that fiction has three key elements: a beginning, middle, and an end. That seems simple enough. These are sometimes referred to as Acts I, II, and III. Acts I and III (the beginning and end) are critical pieces of the story, but are relatively short. Act II holds the guts of the story, where the majority of the action takes place.

The beginning of a story is called the "hook." How do you best capture your readers' interest? Many authors, surprisingly, don't start at the beginning. Instead, their books start with a bang, right in the middle of the action, with the hero embroiled in an exciting scene. Only after the scene's action is resolved do we take a step back and reveal the major characters and setting. Remember, character is action. By starting with an action scene, we automatically learn something about the main character.

Three Key Elements of Fiction
Act I - Beginning—Introduction
Act II - Middle—Rising Action
Act III - End—Falling Action/Resolution

To Outline or Not?

Many writers create outlines of their story, right down to a scene-by-scene description of the action and each character's part in it. Sometimes they use notecards, which can be shuffled around until all the scenes are arranged just the way they want them.

Other authors shun outlines. They start with an idea, add a strong character or two, and then let their storytelling sense guide them along the way. These authors argue that rigid outlines stifle creativity.

So, who's right? They both are. Great works of fiction have been written using both methods. But be warned that people who don't use outlines usually have to go back and do much more editing and revising after their first drafts are finished. Outlines provide a nice roadmap for beginning writers. Don't think of an outline as a rigid pathway; you can make changes along the way, and you probably will. But at least you've got a guide to help steer your story toward a satisfying conclusion.

Hero's Journey

After the beginning, how do you establish the plot and tie it all together? In *The Hero With a Thousand Faces*, author Joseph Campbell described patterns that are common to almost all works of fiction. They form a structure that authors use to tell the same basic tale, a story about a hero who goes on a quest to find a prize and bring it back to his or her tribe.

Some writers think it's useful to keep this "hero's journey" in mind as they dream up their own stories. Of course, you don't have to rigidly follow the structure. It is merely a guide. But if you really study the books and movies you enjoy, you'll discover many of the following elements hidden within.

Left: What kind of journey will your hero take?

Act I

The Ordinary World

This section introduces the hero before the adventure begins. Typical stories show the hero in his or her "normal" world, before a creeping evil upsets the balance of all things. Time spent in the ordinary world allows the writer to identify what the hero wants, and what's at stake.

Above: In *I am Legend,* a cancer cure goes horribly wrong. The resulting plague turns humans into zombie-like victims. Scientist Robert Neville (Will Smith) searches for a solution.

The Call to Adventure

This is where some sort of event happens that gets the story moving. There may be a message or temptation that calls your hero to act. Maybe an asteroid from another planet lands in a nearby farm field. In horror, a warning is often delivered by a type of character, or archetype, called a herald, or a wise old man or woman.

Crossing the Threshold

This is the point where the hero makes a decision (or a decision is made for him), and he's thrown into the adventure. A critical event called a plot point occurs. The hero's world is threatened, or changed, and it's up to the hero to make things right.

Right: When Neville's family is killed, he stays in New York searching for a cure or other survivors.

Act II

Tests and Conflict

Act II is for testing the hero. What allies are met? What enemies? Who is the chief villain, and what are his goals? Does our hero act alone, or is there a group, a posse?

Act II is a series of rising actions and mini-climaxes. In real life, events happen in seemingly random order. But in a good story, each event the hero encounters is connected, leading to the next ordeal.

The Crisis

The crisis is a point in the story where the hero faces his most fearsome test yet, perhaps even enduring a brush with death. It's the "dragging the hero through the gutter" scene, where the hero's faith in himself is put to the ultimate test. Then the hero makes a realization, or figures out a puzzle, and sets off for the final conflict.

Above: Neville is tested. Except for his dog, he's alone. All his attempts to treat victims have failed.

Engage Your Senses

Russian novelist Anton Chekhov once said, "Don't tell me the moon is shining; show me the glint of light on broken glass." Use all your senses. Is there a hint of sweetness to the air, or is it stale? What sound does the wind make when it blows through a darkened woods? Show, don't tell.

Above: In his final struggle, Neville comes face-to-face with a zombie-like victim of the plague.

Act III

The Final Struggle

This is the point in the story where the hero uses everything he's learned and faces the ultimate test. In many horror stories, the conflict becomes a physical action; the final struggle is a fight of some kind, using a combination of physical skills and magic learned during the quest.

Build Suspense

It's always best if your character wins the conflict on his own, especially if he uses skills learned during the course of the story. Beware of having another character swoop in to save the day. This kind of ending is called a *deus ex machina*, a Latin phrase that means "machine of the gods."

How To Build Suspense:

- Add a "ticking clock," a deadline that must be met.
- Keep the action moving.
- Introduce red herrings— false clues that misdirect the reader.
- Use cliffhangers at the end of chapters.

In some ancient Greek plays, a cage with an actor portraying a god inside was lowered onto the stage, where he would miraculously solve the hero's seemingly hopeless problems.

You've probably read books or watched movies where a similar event happened: an unexpected person or situation arises and saves the day. This is what some critics refer to as a contrived ending. Don't resort to this! You've spent the whole story building up your hero with new wisdom and skills. Let him save himself. Otherwise, what's the point of telling your story?

The Return

In many stories, the hero finally returns to his normal world. He brings back a prize, a symbolic magical elixir that benefits his people. Maybe it's gold, or medicine, or simply the head of the monster. But whatever the prize, what really matters is how the hero has changed (or didn't change) during his epic journey.

Above: At the end of a story, heros may return to their normal world. Sometimes they bring back a prize, such as a magic elixir that benefits the people.

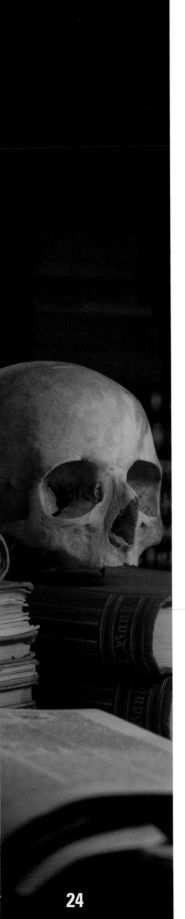

REWRITING

"It is perfectly okay to write garbage—as long as you edit brilliantly."

—C.J. Cherryh

So, you finally finished your story. Congratulations! Whether it's a short story or a novel, you've achieved something most people only dream of. Take a step back, celebrate a little, and then get ready for more work, because there's a truth that you will soon discover: writing is rewriting. Editing your work is a crucial part of the entire process.

Don't edit yourself until you've cranked all the way through your story. If you edit while you write, you'll find things you don't like. It will stifle your creativity as you struggle to make things "perfect." Get that first draft done, then go back and edit.

First, set your story aside for a couple weeks, or at least a few days. Amazingly, with fresh eyes you'll catch mistakes that snuck under your radar the first time around. Your second draft will be better than your first. Your third draft will be an even bigger improvement. Edit and polish your story until it shines. How many drafts do you need? It depends on the story. Some authors do a dozen drafts, others are content with only one or two drafts of editing after the first. You're done when you know in your heart that you've written your story to the very best of your ability.

If you're a writer, then you know the importance of good grammar and spelling. There's no substitute for carefully proofing the story with your own two eyes.

Examine your plot. Are the characters well formed? Do they grow and change? Most important, is your hero likeable? Does the hero have traits we admire? Can we identify with him or her? Do we care if the hero succeeds?

What about the beginning of your book? Does it grab the reader by the throat and never let go?

Are there scenes or events that are really necessary to push the story forward? Be honest with yourself. Be ruthless. Your story will be stronger the tighter you make it. Always, always remember your readers.

Keep your paragraphs short.

When appropriate, use active verbs instead of passive verbs. Instead of "The vampire was struck by the sunlight," try "The sunlight struck the vampire." See how much more immediate and interesting that simple change made the sentence?

Make sure you keep one point of view per scene. If you start focused on one character, stay focused on that character until the end of the scene.

Read your dialogue out loud. Does it sound natural? Does each character have his or her own "voice"?

Left: Use active verbs, such as "The sunlight struck the vampire." Actor Christopher Lee may realize his time is up in *Dracula A.D. 1972.*

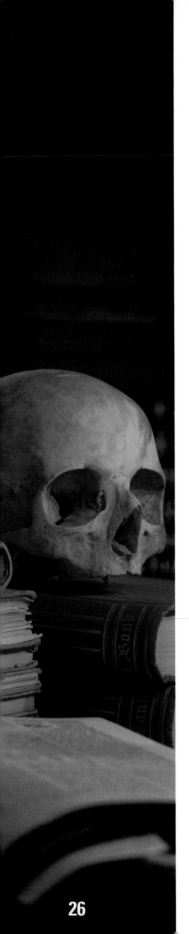

Get Published

"The reason 99 percent of all stories written are not bought by editors is very simple. Editors never buy manuscripts that are left on the closet shelf at home."
—John Campbell

Your story is written and edited—now what? There are many web sites that publish work by young writers. Do an Internet search for "horror webzines" to find good sites. Many of these web sites are also terrific places to learn your craft, with free advice from established authors. You won't get paid much (if anything), but it's a way to get your work seen by an enthusiastic audience.

Or, you could start your own web site and publish online yourself. Some authors post the first chapter or two of their books as a free download, then charge a small fee if the reader wants more. Other authors post their entire work online, happy just to receive reader feedback.

Other Options:

- School newspapers or yearbooks. These publications are always hungry for material.
- Local, regional, or national creative-writing contests.
- Creative-writing clubs and workshops. These are a great way to get feedback from other writers. They also give you practice in critiquing others' work, which will improve your own writing.

- Local newspapers and magazines are always looking for new talent, especially if they can get it for cheap. Still, you have to start somewhere, and it's a way to get your work read by a large audience.
- Self publish. With today's page-layout software, it's easier than ever to create your own publication. Make copies for friends and family.

Publishers

If you are determined to have your story accepted by an established book publisher, first make sure your manuscript is ready. A clean, typewritten, double-spaced, mistake-free manuscript will go a long way in making your story stand out from all the rest. There are many "writer's guide" publications, some available at your library, you can use to research horror markets. They can also tell you how to write a query letter. Put your manuscript in a self-addressed stamped envelope (SASE), wish yourself luck, and mail it off. But please don't sit around waiting for a reply. Keep reading and writing!

Final Thoughts

If you receive a rejection letter, don't despair. Everybody gets them! Remember, the publisher isn't rejecting *you*, only your story. Maybe your writing isn't strong enough just yet. Or maybe your writing is fine, but the publisher isn't buying stories like yours at this time. Trends come and go in the marketplace, but don't try to write what you think publishers are  looking for. By the time you finish your book, the fickle public will have moved on to the Next Big Thing. Simply write what you love, and the rest will follow.

You have the gift of storytelling. Sometimes you just need good timing and a little bit of luck. But remember, the more persistent you are, the luckier you'll get. Keep writing!

Advice From Horror Writers

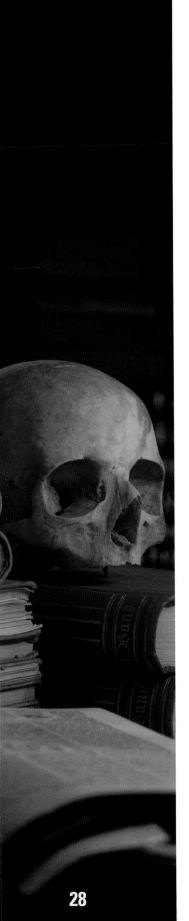

"Writing isn't about making money, getting famous, getting dates... or making friends. In the end, it's about enriching the lives of those who read your work, and enriching your own life, as well."

Stephen King (1947-)

Known as the King of Horror, Stephen King made his mark through clever storytelling in a wonderfully nightmarish way. King has created many horror tales, several of which became successful box office hits.

His second novel, *Salem's Lot*, became his own modern take on the Dracula stories he had read as a boy. In June 1999, while walking alone on a rural Maine road, he was struck by a car. The accident left him in great pain. The popular author thought he'd never write again, but he made an eventual recovery. In 2001, King published *Dreamcatcher*, which included a character recovering from a car wreck. In 2003, the National Book Awards gave King a Lifetime Achievement Award.

"I think everyone likes a good scare, and I think everyone likes to be able to have creepy adventures and face monsters when they know they're safe at the same time."

R.L. Stine (1943-)

As one of the best-selling children's authors of all time, R.L. Stine has more than 300 million books in print. Stine's first teen horror novel, *Blind Date,* became a bestseller in 1986. Soon he was working on *Fear Street,* a series of teenage horror books. Younger kids loved these books, too. The author had a ready audience for his *Goosebumps* books. The first book in the series, *Welcome to Dead House*, was published in 1992. Another 62 books followed, plus a TV series, movies, and even comic books. Some adults said his tales were too frightening for children. But his horror stories helped many kids become avid readers. Said Stine, "I feel happy to terrify kids."

"Sometimes there is no darker place than our thoughts, the moonless midnight of the mind."

Dean Koontz (1945-)

Suspense, terror, excitement, and fear mark best-selling author Dean Koontz's books and life. His youth was marred by an abusive, alcoholic father. At age 8, he set aside his problems to create his own 5¢ hand-written books. Koontz's first published novel, *Star Quest*, came out in 1968. Only three years later, the author was nominated for a Hugo Award for *Beastchild*. Many of Koontz's books feature a madman and a strong woman, characters who were similar to his own father and mother. Koontz's books often end in a happily-ever-after scenario—just like the author's own life. With over a dozen best-selling novels, Koontz's work has been translated into 38 languages.

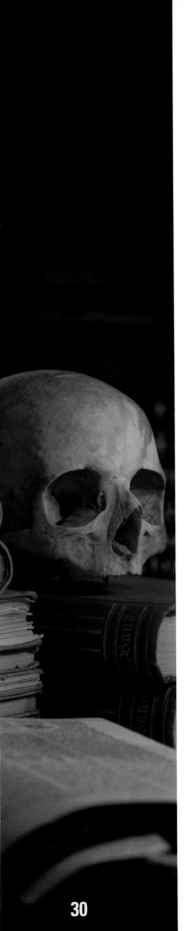

HELPFUL READING

- *On Writing Horror: A Handbook by the Horror Writers Association* edited by Mort Castle

- *How to Write Tales of Horror, Fantasy & Science Fiction* edited by J.N. Williamson

- *The Writer's Journey: Mythic Structure for Writers* by Christopher Vogler

- *The Hero With a Thousand Faces* by Joseph Campbell

- *Stein on Writing* by Sol Stein

- *Self-Editing for Fiction Writers* by Renni Browne and Dave King

- *Writing Dialogue* by Tom Chiarella

- *Building Believable Characters* by Marc McCutcheon

- *Zen in the Art of Writing* by Ray Bradbury

- *The Elements of Style* by William Strunk, Jr., and E.B. White

- *The Transitive Vampire* by Karen Elizabeth Gordon

- *Roget's Super Thesaurus* by Marc McCutcheon

- *2009 Writer's Market* by Robert Brewer

- *Jeff Herman's Guide to Publishers, Editors, & Literary Agents 2009* by Jeff Herman

GLOSSARY

Antagonist — Often called the villain, the antagonist is an important character who tries to keep the hero from accomplishing his or her goal.

Archetype — A type of character that often appears in stories. Archetypes have special functions that move the story along, such as providing the hero with needed equipment or knowledge.

Backstory — The background and history of a story's characters and setting. When writing, it is good to know as much backstory as possible, even if most of it never appears in the final manuscript.

First-Person Viewpoint — The "I" viewpoint, which makes it seem as if the person telling the story is the one who experienced it first-hand. "I grabbed my garlic and turned to meet the vampire," is an example of first-person viewpoint.

Genre — A type, or kind, of a work of art. In literature, a genre is distinguished by a common subject, theme, or style. Some genres include science fiction, fantasy, mystery, and horror.

Hook — The beginning of a story, used to grab a reader's interest.

Plagiarism — To copy somebody else's work.

Point of View — The eyes, or viewpoint, through which we experience a story or scene.

Protagonist — A story's hero or main character. The protagonist propels the story.

Third-Person Viewpoint — A detached, neutral point of view in which the story is told by an all-seeing narrator. "Jane grabbed her garlic. Was a vampire waiting around the corner?" is an example of third-person viewpoint.

INDEX

Right: Who will you scare with your next horror story? Your readers!